Photoshop qui-keys

A quick-step guide for learning Photoshop in less time than it takes for the average nooner.

Copyright Notice

Photoshop qui-keys
A quick-step guide to learning Photoshop in less time than it takes
than your average nooner.

Copyright © 2016 by Phil Jones

RGB Fill – Media & Design
9936 Grey Sea Eagle Ave
Las Vegas, NV 89117
www.madrgbfill.com

Ordering Information:
Quantity sales. Special discounts are available on quantity
purchases by corporations, associations, and others. For details,
contact the publisher at the address above.
Orders by U.S. trade bookstores and wholesalers. Please contact
Kindle Books or Amazon.com.

Cover Art by Phil Jones

About the Author

Over 25 years ago, I started dabbling in graphic design, only I didn't realize it and back then it was referred to desktop publishing. With my OCR type ball firmly in place in the old IBM Selectric III, I began placing clip art with text and created the MOD (Message Of the Day) for my Navy training center in Dam Neck, Virginia.

It took me nearly 20 years to realize that graphic design was my calling, as one design job or another had always fallen into my lap throughout the years. At that time, in 2004, I decided to get my Bachelor's degree in one of the graphic design fields, Visual Effects and Motion Graphics. While I haven't done much in the way of that, I have stayed on top the design field, honing and perfecting my skills with every chance I get.

Within just a few short years of graduating, I was given the opportunity to instruct at one of the design schools where I live - The International Academy of Design & Technology (now Sanford Brown), and taught there for several years.

Currently, after merging my ability to teach with my passion for design and typography, I'm striking out on my own. Writing my first book is the beginning of putting my new mantra in to practice - "Learn, Do, Teach". Every day we have the opportunity to learn something new, do what we love and teach what we've learned. I believe this isn't only an obligation to ourselves, but that it is our obligation to society to making future generations better than ours.

Preface

For years now, people have told me to write a book on the tips and tricks I've shared with them in their educational and design goals. I never did listen to them, until now, and my goal is to help budding artists, designers and entrepreneurs quickly learn from my years of experience.

What lead me down this road to writing the proceeding book is the fact that all my current clientele are published authors, and I thought "I can do that". So, here we are, praise to drive me forward, pen to paper, and the firm belief that what follows will have anybody dabbling in Photoshop up and running with confidence and speed in just a short amount of time.

The tips and tricks I'm sharing in this e-book with you are a variety of shortcuts and quick keys that will help with your work flow, speed up the design process and build your confidence with the program. A lot of these shortcuts can be utilized in the other Adobe© design software. Also, through my choice of words, I'll be sharing ways for remembering the keys and what they do. I hope you get everything you need out of this book and quickly be on your way to becoming a design enthusiast or professional.

Phil Jones
BS, MFA, Designer, Author

Table of Contents

The Difference Between Art & Design:

Good art sends a different message
to everyone.

Good design sends the same message
to everyone.

Beginning with The Basics.

Command & Control
aka Cmd + Ctrl

The **Cmd** key on a Mac and the **Ctrl** key on a PC are perhaps the two most important keys you'll need to remember and become familiar with in your design skills. Whether you personally use a Mac or a PC, these two keys form the basis for many other shortcuts and are often interchanged during conversations or training videos out there. It is for these reasons that, as an avid designer or a budding professional, everyone should know these two keys by heart and get a *feel* for them on the keyboard.

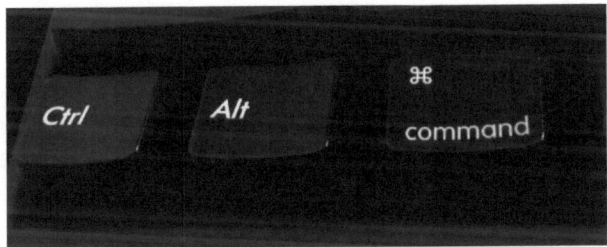

Shift + Alt

The Shift and Alt keys are the second most common keys you'll need to become familiar with in learning Photoshop or design in general. These two keys, for now, allow you to either select sub-menus within a set or to accomplish multiple functions at once. We will go into more detail later as we look at specific commands or key combos that I find essential to the design process.

OMG!
There's so many panels.

Don't fret, mon petit! This too can be broken down into three easy parts. First, for this to be accurate as possible, these panels you're seeing (hopefully not for the first time) should be the default or Essentials panel preset that is one of many presets that Adobe© offers. If you are opening Photoshop for the first time, you can quickly check this by looking at the top right corner of your window. Just below, or to the right of the ▬ ☐ X is a drop-down menu, clicking on it will allow you to change or reset your workspace to the Essentials preset. Now, back to the basics of what you're seeing in the opened program.

1 Left Panel (tools)

The left panel set is your main design set. Whether you're drawing, selecting, refining or enhancing, most of the tools you'll be using are located here...in case you forget the shortcut.

2 Right Panel (type & color)

The right set of tools will allow you to change fonts, input special characters (also known as glyphs or symbols) and work with your paragraph spacing and indents. It also allows you to quick select colors or ranges of color.

3 Top Panel (adjust and modify)

The third, and top panel allow you to make adjustments to your actively selected tool. This can be anything from color, to brush type, size and more. We'll get more into this later.

The Layers Panel
(your project bin)

The Layers panel is the project bin for the file you're working on. Everything that you import, shapes that you create or type that you add will be located in your project bin. The order goes from top to bottom and you can think of it as transparencies from the old days of overhead AV projectors. If you're too young to know what those are, look it up (insert emoji here).

The need-to-knows here are that you can adjust how top layers interact with the layer directly below it. These are known as Layer Adjustments and we'll talk more on this in the next few chapters. The other need-to-knows are the active layer will be highlighted. Right clicking on a highlighted layer will bring up additional options that are available for that layer. Each layer also has an eyeball icon to the left. Clicking this will view/hide the layer.

There is a lot more you need to know about this panel, but that is covered in the chapter labeled "Layers Panel". You can jump there now if you want. The take away here is pay attention to this panel. If you're not mindful of which layer you're on, you can place elements

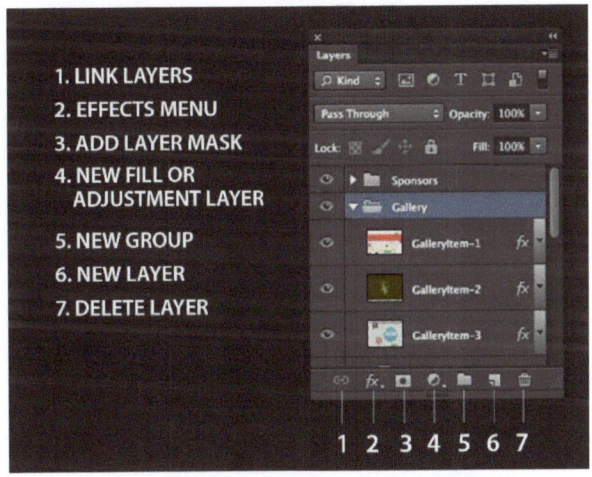

1. LINK LAYERS
2. EFFECTS MENU
3. ADD LAYER MASK
4. NEW FILL OR ADJUSTMENT LAYER
5. NEW GROUP
6. NEW LAYER
7. DELETE LAYER

where they don't belong, accidentally hide them behind other layers or accidentally and negatively affect one layer when you meant to perform that step to a different one. When in doubt, check your layers panel. Look for the highlighted or active layer.

3

Tip #1

If a tool isn't working, or nothing is happening with the tool you think you have active, chances are another tool or command sequence isn't completed. Hit "Enter" on your keyboard to exit the current state and gain access to the correct tool or layer.

Basic
Quick Keys

V = mo_V_e tool, your default tool

M = _M_arquee tool - makes a selection or defines an area.

L = _L_asso tool, also used for defining areas.

T = _T_ype tool, allows you to type and define an area for type.

E = _E_ye Dropper, lets you sample an area for matching colors.

C = _C_rop tool, let's you Cut an image's size

G = _G_radient tool, lets you place a gradient of colors into an area.

W = magic _W_and, allows you to select an area based on color.

P = _P_en tool, allows you to draw shapes or define areas.

A = Selection tool, lets you select an object or an _A_nchor point.

The Left Panel Toolset.

The Digital Designer's Tool Kit

At the end of the last chapter, I gave you a basic list of quick keys. At the beginning of the chapter, I told you that shift and/or alt allow you to navigate sub-menus or to perform multiple actions at once. Here is where the two come together to make the design process much easier. With the main tool bar, as it's also called, holding down shift or tapping shift will cycle through the available variations of that tool. While you can always click on a tool to expand its toolset, using Shift + "Letter Key" is a much quicker process and keeps you from mousing across your screen and work area...which can also reduce accidental errors such as moving a layer.

Most of the tools have toolsets available using the Shift + Key option, however, there are also additional tools that may not be available, as indicated in the Marquee tool graphic provided. If using the Shift + Key option doesn't provide a tool that you think should be available in that toolset, click on the menu item's carrot to see all available tools within the toolset.

Also, with each tool you use, you will have to do one of two things to exit that tool and select another. The first and most common is to hit Enter on your keyboard. This confirms the action and allows you to proceed. The second is Ctrl or Cmd + D to De-select the area. This is most common when you've made a selection with any of the area selecting tools.

Area defining tools quick keys:
M = <u>M</u>arquee tool   L = <u>L</u>asso tool   W = magic <u>W</u>and

The Left Panel Toolset.

Clicking on the tool's carrot will expand the toolset.

Pressing M on your keyboard will select the Marquee tool.

Tapping Shift + M will select the Elliptical Marquee tool.

The two single row Marquees options aren't part of the quick-key function.

Toolsets with a Shift + Key option will have a corresponding letter next to it, as in the diagram.

Tip #2

Any tool in the tools panel that has multiple tools in the toolset will have a "carrot" next to it in the bottom right corner. It can be seen as a triangle or arrow pointing down and to the right. Click on this to manually expand the toolset and to explore other options.

V
The Default Tool

If you're ever lost, and if you're just starting out on the path of design and Photoshop, you will be lost quite often. Even after years of experience, I still flub things up, leave things unfinished or accidentally hit a key and have no clue what I just activated. That being said, whenever you're lost, simply hit V on your keyboard. V, or the moVe tool is your default, go to, always start with me tool. There are only two instances where you can't hit V and get back to home-base. These are if you're actively typing in a text box, or, you have not committed to the previous action by hitting Enter / Cmd / Ctrl + D to deselect. In either case, the solution is easy and is as follows:

1 Gray Zones (for typing and/or active text box)

If you have an active text box open, hitting V on your keyboard will only result in VVVVVV running across your screen. Simply move your mouse to the gray zone between your image/file and the tool panels and click your mouse. This releases the text box and allows you to return to the default tool.

2 Commit (a mystery tool is still active)

Photoshop demands that you commit to your current action. Whether selecting an area or transforming a layer by altering its scale, rotation or whatever, once you start an action you have to finish it. The only way Photoshop allows you to do this is by hitting Enter on your keyboard. Believe me, after a while, YOU WILL want to hit your keyboard.

When working in Photoshop, if you're not drawing (using the Pen Tool or other shape tools) or painting using any of the Brush tools, you should always be in the default tool – which is shortcut V or clicking on the moVe tool. It is the first tool in your tools panel and is required to be active to use some of the other features.

The Left Panel Toolset.

Cmd + Ctrl Keys
That will save the day

Now that you know enough to be a danger to your own design...or to other designers, let me share with you some more quick keys that can literally save the project and your ass. I can't tell you how many times I've been saved by knowing them by heart and using them faithfully.

Command & Control
Shortcuts

For sake of discussion, I'm only using the Mac controls. If you are using a PC, please remember that Cmd is replaced with Ctrl in the quick keys.

Cmd + S
Saves your project. I highly recommend you do this every 5-10 minutes. Make it a habit, it will save your day!

Cmd + Shift + S
Saves a copy of your project. If you need to show the current state of your work as a JPEG, this is the way to go.

Cmd + Z
Undoes your last move. If you flub up or just don't like the result, undo your move with this quick key. This is only good for one go-back though.

Cmd + Shift + Z
Undoes up to 10 (more or less) of your errors, disliked results or your general dissatisfaction. Great if you have to go back more than one move.

Cmd + X
Deletes the selected object, layer or item.

Cmd + T
Allows you to transform aspects of the selected object such as scale and rotation.

3 Ways
To Make a Selection

I've talked a bunch about making a selection and the tools you can use to do so. But, I haven't actually told you how these tools differ or the process of making a selection. So...where do I begin? First, the ants have to go marching one by one...no, just kidding, but there are marching ants involved. With any of the selection tools, you'll know your selection is complete because there will be little dashes on your screen that appear to be moving...hence the name "marching ants". If you don't see these after making a selection, you haven't closed your selection area. What this means is, whatever point you start from in defining an area, you have to end in that same exact spot. For the most part. Using the Magic Wand is different, but you will still see marching ants.

The Lasso Tool and the Marquee Tool both allow you to drag and/or draw your selection across the screen, defining an area to be modified somehow in a future step. The

Magic Wand tool is different in that you select color ranges instead of defined areas of interest. Here are some of their basic differences:

1 Lasso Tool (freeform)

The Lasso Tool allows you to define an area either by holding your left mouse key down continuously while dragging across your screen to define an area. If using the Polygon Lasso Tool you'll define an area by clicking at different points around the canvas you're wanting to define. With both tools of the set, the beginning and ending anchor points need to connect.

2 Marquee Tool (pre-defined)

The Marquee Tool only allows you to make a selection within the general shape of the tool in the set. So, the *square* Marquee Tool allows for rectangular selections and the *round* Marquee Tool is for elliptical selections. This method automatically encloses the defined area, but is more limited by shape. It often the right tool for the job though.

3 Magic Wand (color stops)

The Magic Wand only lets you select areas based on color. To refine or add to your selection, you simply click on more colors of the area to be defined. You know when a swatch of color, or color stop, is selected because the marching ants will be active. This can be used from subtle gradients to highly contrasting images.

When you have an area selection tool active, you can modify or refine the selection by adding to it or subtracting areas from your original selection. To do this, you will need to select the appropriate modifier in the Top Panel toolset. We will discuss this panel in more detail later. Suffice it to say that when a selection tool is active, the top panel will display – on the left side – three little marching ant icons that correspond to add, subtract and merge. Hover over each one to see a hint pop up that prompts what the modifier function will do.

The Right
Panel Toolset.

History, Character
and Color

No...it's not what you think. The Right Panel toolset is where you can find panels to view your session History, control your Characters (and paragraphs) and choose or define Colors to use on the canvas. It also allows you to make adjustments to your paint brushes, but this is more in-depth and I'd like to reserve that for a future book.

There are also things here called "actions" which are automated scripts that create specific looking end products, usually 3d in nature. These too are more advanced and while I encourage you to look through and explore the Photoshop program, Actions are beyond the scope of coverage for this e-book. Perhaps that will be in my next book.

Perhaps the most important panel in the Right Toolset area is the History Panel. Clicking on it will expand the view and allow you to see recent changes to your document. Clicking on any of the visible layers in the History panel gives you the opportunity to revert to a previous state of your document. Think of them as snapshots. Each time you make a change to your document, a snapshot is entered into the History panel. Clicking on one will *gray out* any of the snapshots below it. While in the History panel, you can go forward or backward in time as many times as you'd like. Making any changes to the physical document (not the History panel snapshots) will create a new time line from the snapshot you were on in the History panel. Doing this will wipe out or erase any snapshots that were below that point in time in History.

The Right Panel Toolset.

The History Panel - snapshots of your document from the beginning to its most current state.

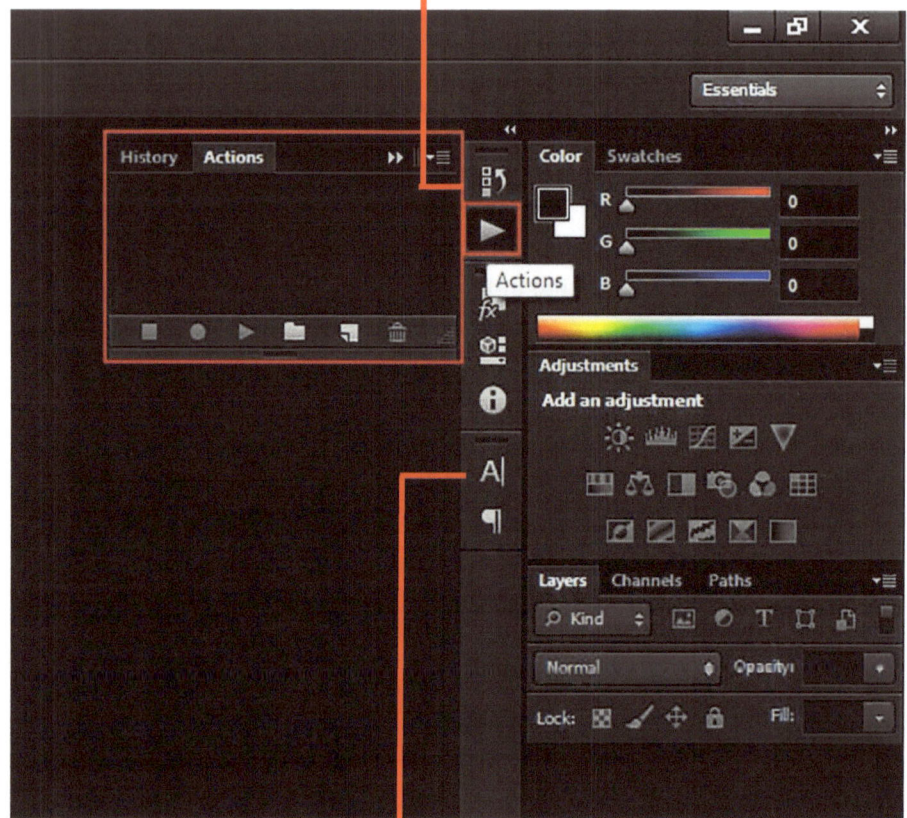

The Character Panel – used for font choices, line spacing options, select all caps or lower case and much more.

Besides the all-important History Panel in this toolset is the Character Panel. The Character panel allows you to have more control over your type in your document. Some of the features here are the ability to change or scroll through fonts, change the size of the font, use of all caps or all lower-case letters, increase or decrease the spacing between lines of text and much more. If you're serious about becoming a designer, Character Panel needs to become one of your new best friends. Get to know everything about it.

Here are some examples of the History Panel as mentioned in the beginning of this chapter.

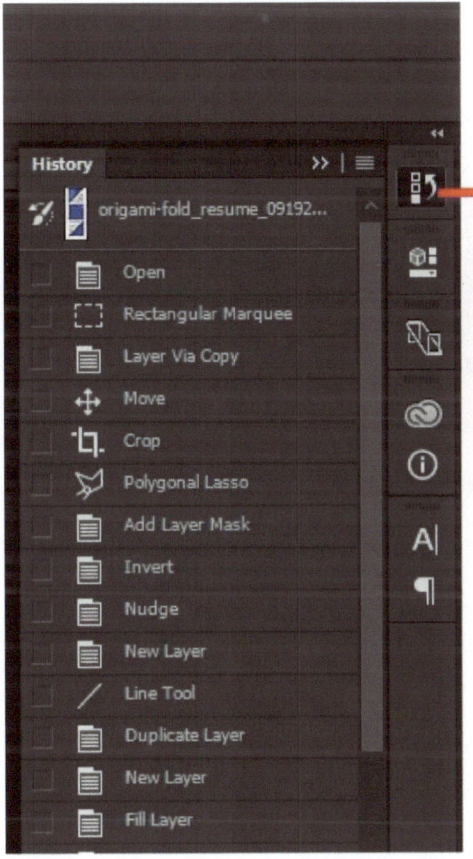

When the History Panel is expanded, it reveals *snapshots* of the changes made to your document.

Important note: The snapshots are listed in descending order. This means the most recent change is at the bottom of the panel and the oldest changes are located at the top.

The Right Panel Toolset.

Tip #3

Cmd + Z or Cmd + Shift + Z are ways to undo your last move or series of moves. The History Panel allows you to move in time, which is different than the Cmd + Z function. Designers often start with the Z function and then move to the History Panel if necessary.

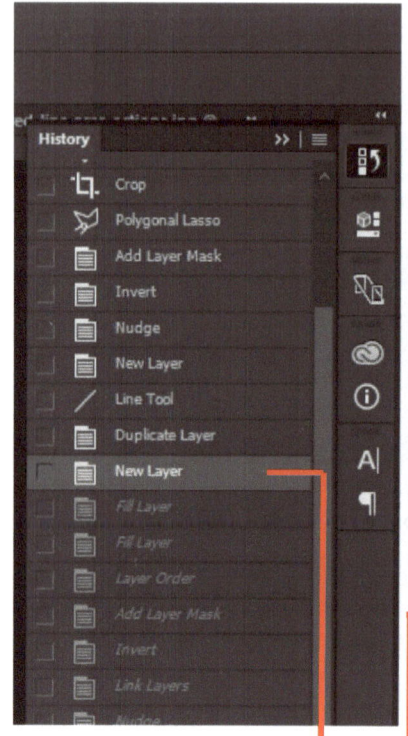

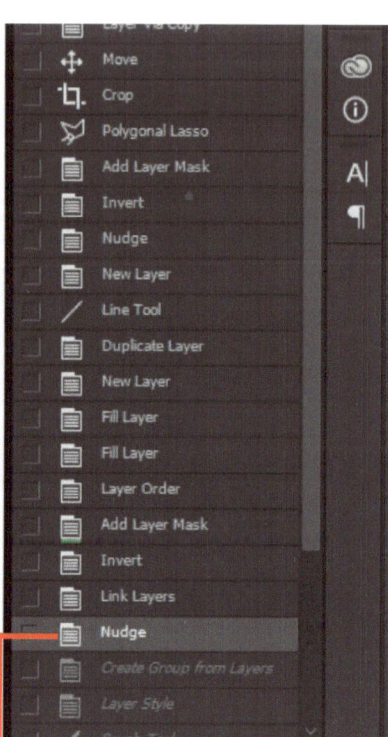

Clicking on a layer in the History Panel reverts your document to that previous state. All the layers below it will become *grayed out*.

Before making any new changes to your actual document, you can move forward or backwards by clicking in the time line.

The Top
Panel Toolset.

Support for
The Left Panel

The Top Panel toolset provides support for the tools in the Left Panel toolset. Clicking on any one of the Left Panel tools will bring up a new menu along the top. While there are too many to define here and now, I encourage you to explore the Top Panel toolset as you click through each of the tools in the Left Panel. I will attempt to provide some basics here for you to get started with and highlight some f the differences in choices that may seem to provide the same function at first glance.

Cmd + T (transform)

The support panel allows you to rotate, scale or distort the object selected. While you can usually do this from within your working area, sometimes images or objects are so large that custom inputs are quicker and easier.

Selection Tools (M, L, W)

When using any of your selection tools, Marquee, Lasso and Magic Wand, the support menu gives you options to control the harshness or softness of the edge of the selection (aka feathering). It also allows you to add to or subtract from selections or to make a union of two selections. The nice thing is that you can start with one selection tool and move between them seamlessly to define and refine your selected area.

Area defining tools quick keys:

M = <u>M</u>arquee tool   L = <u>L</u>asso tool   W = magic <u>W</u>and

Brush Tools (B, J, S, Y)

Ok, not to rude or insensitive, but there's a mnemonic to remember your brush tools, and that is "BJ's...why?" Whether you love them or hate them (not the BJ's you're thinking of), brushes are a big part of Photoshop. The basics here though are on flow, opacity and brush hardness. Opacity and Flow are similar, but think of them like an air gun and the canvas. Flow is *how much* pigment is being allowed to *reach the canvas*. Opacity is *how visible* that color is *on the canvas*. Using flow allows you to make several passes, building up layers of pigment. Selecting the style of the brush and how soft or hard its edges are can be done just below the Edit Menu. Each Brush tool works slightly different, so I recommend experimenting to familiarize yourself with all of them.

Brush tools quick keys:

B = paint Brush   J = Healing Brush   S = clone Stamp
Y = historY brush

Tip #4

B selects your Brush Tool with your last selected or used brush. The bracket keys [ ] increase or decrease the size of your Brush. To quickly fill your canvas or selected area with the Foreground Color use Alt + Delete and Cmd + Delete for the Background Color.

The Healing Brush tool is the oddball here. When using it, think of Joining (or copying) areas of your canvas. This brush allows you to select an area of one layer to copy and then paints it into a different area of the same layer on the canvas.

Pen Tool - P (draw and define)

The Pen Tool allows you to both define an area by creating a Path or a shaPe. The support menu gives you this option, just make sure to select the right one before drawing its boundaries. You can think of a Path as an imaginary plane defined by its anchor points (where you click your mouse).

Paths can be used to control animation sequences or confine objects (like type) to them. Shapes, on the other hand, are defined areas with a fill (inside color) and/or a stroke (border color). Shapes can serve as design elements or to define areas of text.

Shape Tool - U (pre-defined paths or shapes)

Similar in function to the Pen Tool, the Shape Tool is used to create shapes, paths or Underlines for text but, the shapes or paths are already pre-defined. The support menu allows you to control the path or shape options, as well as stroke and fill values. Think of Underline when using quick keys to access the Shape Tool.

Tip #5

To refine or edit the anchor points of a path or shape hit the A Key to select All your Anchor Points or Shift + A to select a single point. Add more by holding down Cmd while clicking additional points.

When All Else Fails, Drop Down

Above the Support Panel, there is the Menu Bar. Each tab has numerous options in its drop down menu. The tabs themselves are pretty self-explanatory as to what they offer and the functionality of your design and workspace. The following are some of the basic need-to-knows.

File

This is the control center for creating new files (Cmd + N), saving files (Cmd + S), placing files into your existing document or starting a new document from an existing file. If you need to print your image (Cmd + P), this is the place.

Edit

The Edit Menu allows you to edit (go figure) elements of your document. Check spelling, undo mistakes, transform objects or adjust stroke and fill colors of a shape or layer, this is the menu for all your editing functions.

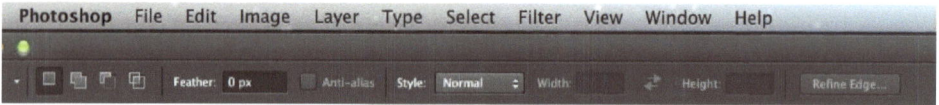

Image

When you import an image into Photoshop, you may need to make adjustments to it. All of your image adjusting controls can be found here. To change brightness, enhance colors or to make something look old-timey, use the Image panel dropdown.

Layer

The Layer Menu controls or adjusts the layers in your project bin or Layers Panel. Remember that area on the right that I told you about in chapter 1? Here, you can merge layers, export (save) layers, rename, lock or hide. The layers panel controls how selected layers (or parts of layers) interact with each other.

Type

Everything you need to create, edit, modify or enhance your type can be found in this menu. Replacing missing fonts, turning fonts into shapes or to change the language you are typing in can all be found in this menu.

Window

Window controls all the other windows, or tabs in your work area. Sometimes, I have clicked or hit something and a window disappears and I know something like this will happen to you. Simply go to the Window tab and look for the missing window. If it doesn't have a check, check it.

Filter

There really is no explaining this one in a quick-step guide. Filters can take a book on their own, and a very thick book at that. If you're goal is to make an image look like a charcoal drawing or text/type to look like plastic or glass, then the Filter tab is where you'll find those effects. Discovery, time and practice is the only thing I can tell you about the Filters tab, in this book.

Help

If you're new to Photoshop, I'm sure you'll get lost and need some help. Adobe is great at customer support and their Help Menu is full of advice and support. Use this menu as a first means to find a solution to your problem. If you can't find the answer, Adobe community chat boards are a great next step in the learning and discovery process.

A Lot
To Take In

Yeah, I know...that was a lot to take in. But, we're over the hump now. Now, it's almost time to sit back and take a cool drag off a cigarette and bask in the glory of making Photoshop your bia...you get the idea.

Photoshop, and all of Adobe's software, are large, complicated and cumbersome mules...but when they get you to where you want to go, you're thankful you had them to get you there. I hope I've been able to break down the initial barriers and shock to get you up and running and wanting to design. Whether for personal, educational, entrepreneurial or professional development, Photoshop can be tamed and mastered. Here's a quick re-cap of the Top Menu Bar and Support Panel that we've discussed so far.

1 Top Menu Bar

The Top Menu Bar is your go-to source for tools, commands or actions that affect your images, layers or type and gives you options to save, export and print your files. Special effects like oil painting, plastic or glass can be added to images or type through the Filter panel. If a tool panel or tab disappears, you only need to look at the Windows Panel to see what is checked or unchecked to fix the problem. When all else fails, use the Help tab, Adobe has great support and a tight community.

2 Support Panel

The Support Panel, just below the Menu Bar, allows you to modify or customize tools selected in the Left Tools Panel. Each tool has its own features. Brushes have flow and opacity controls as well as different types of brushes with soft or hard edges. Selection Tools have add,

subtract and union features to define and refine the
area(s) being selected.

Path or ShaPe tools let you easily draw custom shapes,
place predefined shapes and adjust height, scale or
width as well as rotating an object by manually inputting
information.

The Top Panel, or support panel, is the place to go when the tool you're
using isn't *easily* allowing you to perform the task. Whether it's defining the
number of points of a star or the sides of a polygon, all of the control options
will be found here. I recommend you select a path or shape defining tool and
experiment with the Top Panel.

The Canvas,
Or Work Area.

Putting Everything
You've Learned into Practice

Now that you know what the different panels are used for, it's time you put everything into practice. I would be remiss if I left out some basic information on how to actually draw a marquee selection and what it means to hover, drag or swap colors. While some of this may be extremely basic for some of you, this is a basic or beginning manual, so I feel it is important to discuss some of these key terms when it comes to working in the canvas area of Photoshop.

The Canvas

Just to be sure that everyone is on the same page, the Canvas is that area of the screen between all your tools and panels. When you create or open a document, it will appear here, in the middle of your screen.

Foreground & Background (aka Stroke & Fill)

When looking at the Left Tool Panel, at the bottom you'll see two colors, these are your Foreground and Background colors. When, however, you're working with a shape - such as a square - these then become the Fill and Stroke colors. Fill refers to color on the inside of a shape and Stroke refers to the edge or outside color.

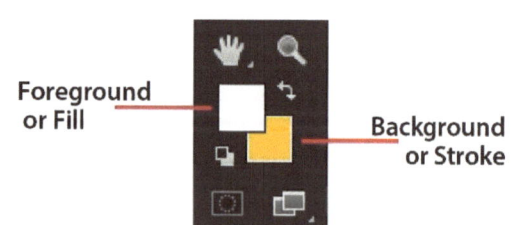

Foreground or Fill

Background or Stroke

Click Alt Shift Drag Release

Yes, as a budding designer, you will have to do all that - and more. When working with the Marquee Selection tool or the Shape Tool, you will have to Click + Drag and then release the left mouse button after drawing your selection area on the canvas.

To add upon this technique, Click + Alt + Drag, creates your selection but scales it out from the center of where you initially clicked. Going one step further, when you make a selection by (left) Click + Alt + Shift + Drag, you not only scale out your selection from the center but also constrain its proportions. This means its height and width are kept equal to one another. Now, for the icing on the cake...when you add Spacebar to the mix, you can move your selection around the canvas to refine its position. So, that's Click + Alt + Shift + Drag + Spacebar...all before you release the mouse key. It is very important you keep the left mouse key pressed while performing this action. Releasing the mouse will end the sequence and you may have to define your selection all over again. Here's the recap:

Click + Drag
Allows you to draw a selection or shape to the canvas.

Click + Alt + Drag
Draws your selection from the center point out.

Click + Alt + Shift + Drag
Constrains the proportions of the shape.

Click + Alt + Shift + Drag + Space
Moves the shape while drawing.

Tip #6

Releasing the left mouse key while making a selection or drawing a predefined shape will end the function you are performing. When using the Pen Tool or Polygon Lasso Tool, you have to click and release to add anchor points to your selection while starting and stopping at the same point to end or close the selection. To add to or refine a selection, use the Top Panel for refining options.

Using all these keys at once may be confusing or difficult at first, to say the least, but with a little practice it will become second nature. **Click + Alt + Shift + Drag + Space** is the most difficult because dragging defines the area to be selected. Activating the Spacebar while dragging temporarily pauses the defining function and allows the already defined area to be moved on the canvas. Releasing the Spacebar re-enables the selection tool to further define a selection.

A Word
On Layers.

Blending Modes,
Masks and Layer Effects

The last thing I think budding designers should know is how to work with and modify layers in the layers panel or project bin.

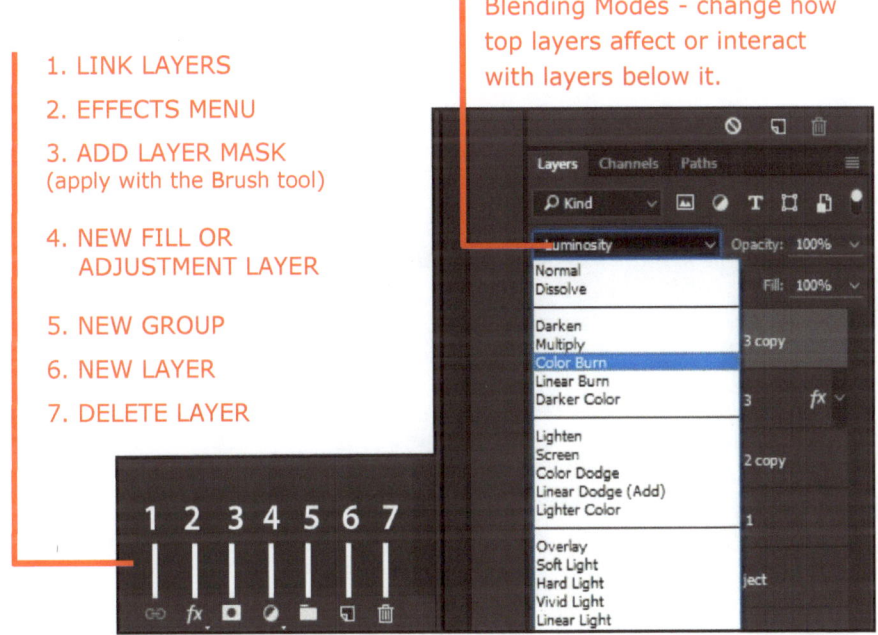

Blending Modes - change how top layers affect or interact with layers below it.

1. LINK LAYERS

2. EFFECTS MENU

3. ADD LAYER MASK
(apply with the Brush tool)

4. NEW FILL OR
   ADJUSTMENT LAYER

5. NEW GROUP

6. NEW LAYER

7. DELETE LAYER

Blending modes are how your layers interact or blend with each other. I encourage you to create two or three layers and explore the different outcomes by selecting different blending modes. Also, play around with adding effects (#2) on text layers or shape layers.

The Canvas or Work Area.

The bottom tool bar allows you to trash layers, create new layers and mask out parts of layers. Masks simply use white or black to reveal or hide sections of your layer. Clicking on the Mask icon will add it to the selected layer. One of the nice thing about using masks is that you can remove unwanted elements from the image/layer without destroying the original. Think of it as turning the lights on or off. When the lights are off, or blacked out, you can't see anything, When the lights are on, everything that was there is still there, just now it's being revealed.

In Closing,
Some Afterthoughts.

So Much to Learn,
So Little Time.

While your brain may be ready to explode at this point, I hope that you've been able to crack the code of using Photoshop and I have begun to help you demystify it.

Photoshop takes some time to get used to it, more time to really enjoy it and years to master it...if you ever can truly master an ever evolving and expanding program. That being said, it really is a great program and I hope that anybody that has an inkling of design sense has the opportunity to understand its function and develops a love-hate relationship with using it. I say this jokingly, because I do love the program. Unfortunately, as with any program, things can and will go wrong at the worst possible moment.

When things go horribly wrong, and they will, remember that if you get in the practice of saving your work every five minutes or so, you can alleviate a lot of the stress, headaches and oh (expletive deleted) moments that will follow the unexpected program crash.

I plan on creating more of these quick-step guides for Photoshop and some of the other design programs. I welcome and invite you to provide feedback on the site wherever you purchased my e-book. Through your comments, I can edit, add and create content you're searching for and deliver it in a package that takes less than an hour to digest it, instead of the days, weeks or months it normally can take. After all, who wants a three-month commitment when all you have time for is a nooner? Thanks for reading and look for my up and coming books.

Notes

Appendix: A
Basic Qui-keys & Their Function.

V – Move   Used to move the selected item.

M - Marquee Selection   Used to select an area in an elliptical or rectangular shape.

L - Lasso Tool   Used to select an area by dragging your mouse OR by clicking points on your canvas.

W - Magic Wand   Used to select an area based on color.

C - Crop Tool   Used to crop or cut your selection without changing resolution.

E - Eye Dropper   Used to sample a color for color matching or adding to your color swatches.

B - Paint Brush   Selects the default or last defined paint brush to *paint* color onto the canvas.

G - Gradient Tool   Used to place a range of colors onto your canvas in a linear, radial or reflected direction.

P - Pen Tool   Used to draw custom shapes or define custom areas on the canvas via shape & path.

T - Type Tool   Dragging will define a text area and/or place a blinking prompt for you to begin typing.

A - Direct Selection

Used to select All or One of the anchor points of the active path or shape to move or refine.

U -Shape Tool

Used to draw a pre-defined shape or Underline areas of text.

H - Hand Tool

Used to pan large images across the screen without moving elements on the canvas.

Z - Zoom Tool

Used to zoom in or out on your canvas to see the big picture or minute details. (Use ALT+ Z to zoom out)

X

Used to swap your Foreground and Background colors.

D

Used to reset Foreground and Background colors to the defaults of white and black.

Appendix: B
Basic Shortcuts & Their Function

PC users will have to substitute Cmd for Ctrl on their keyboards.

Cmd + A	Selects All.
Cmd + J	Copies the selection & places in new layer.
Cmd + Shift + J	Cuts the selection & places in new layer.
Cmd + T	Activates layer to be Transformed.
Cmd + Shift + T	Rotates the active object or layer in 15% increments.
Cmd + S	Saves the file as a Photoshop document or the last saved file type.
Cmd + Shift + S	Prompts to save as different file types.
Cmd + X	Extracts active layer or object and deletes it.
Cmd + Z	*Un-duhZ* your last action.
Cmd + Alt + Z	Undoes the last several actions.
Cmd + D	De-selects the selected area (Marching Ants).
Cmd + N	Creates a New document.
Cmd + E	Merges Everything, selected or highlighted, into one layer.

Appendix: C
Basic Design Language

As you begin to design, you'll need to know some of the basic language professional designers use.

Kerning The spacing between individual letters.

Tracking The spacing between words in one line of text.

Leading The spacing between lines or rows of text.

White Space The negative space or unused area around design elements on the canvas.

Negative Space The white space or unused area around design elements on the canvas.

Canvas The working area of your design.

Resolution Refers to the number of pixels per inch (ppi) or dots per inch (dpi). 300 dpi is needed for print, 72 dpi is for web.

Format The file type of your image. This could be JPEG, PNG or PDF, just to name a few. Different uses of your design may require different formats.

www.ingramcontent.com/pod-product-compliance
Lightning Source LLC
Chambersburg PA
CBHW050857290526
45792CB00002B/632